Frank Whittle

The Dawn of the Jet Age

Molly Burkett and the pupils of
William Farr Comprehensive School, Welton, Lincoln.

The students would like to thank the following for their help
   Doctor David Bray, Flight Lieutenant Ade Peel,
   Professor Trevor Kerry, Tim Pierce and Cranwell library staff,
   Leonard Morris, Geoff Smith of Lutterworth Museum,
   Ian Whittle, Roy Fowkes, Captain Eric Brown and Ian
   Craighead (Rolls Royce).

Students have had the opportunity to visit R.A.F. Cranwell and work with officers and senior lecturers to understand the principles of flight and the importance of the jet engine. In addition, interviewing techniques have been taught and they have spent time with the librarians of the R.A.F. Cranwell College library learning how to research and record information. They have also worked with writers and been taught the techniques in publishing – editing, proof reading, illustrating, technical drawing, cover design and finally printing.
   We wish them well in their future careers,
      The Cranwell Branch of the Royal Aeronautical Society
         and all of us at Barny Books.

First published by Barny Books
All rights reserved

No part of this publication may be reproduced or transmitted in any way or by any means, including electronic storage and retrieval, without prior permission of the publisher.

ISBN No: 978.1.906542.36.8

Publishers: Barny Books
   Hough on the Hill, Grantham, Lincolnshire. NG32 2BB
   Tel: 01400 250246   www.barnybooks.co.uk

Printers: Spiegl Press Limited
   42 Guash Way, Ryhall Road Industrial Estate
   Stamford, Lincs. PE9 1XH
   Tel: 01780 762550   www.spiegl.co.uk

I was out shooting rooks in North Rauceby Woods when we heard this noise like a grating mangle. We stopped and looked up. There was this aircraft over Cranwell and I knew straight away what it was. We often took young RAF officers with us when we went shooting and we had some of them with us that day. They tried to convince us that they were checking out a new propeller but I knew what they were really checking out, a new type of engine. A boy in our class at school had a father who was a policeman at Cranwell and he was on guard duty at a hangar where they had been working on it. He wasn't supposed to tell anyone about it but he told his son and he told us. All the boys in our class knew what was going on.

Stan Blackbourn

Gerry Sayers ready to take off

We were out on the road when we heard the noise of this aeroplane going over. I knew straight away that there was something wrong with it because it was making this noise and it didn't have a propeller. How could an aeroplane fly without a propeller? It had been a miserable wet day but it had cleared up about an hour earlier. It was my mother's birthday so I will always remember the day, the fifteenth of May.

Mary Bellamy

    The weather was atrocious. I was flying a Martlet from Donibristle, near the Forth Bridge down to Croydon when I hit even stronger winds as I crossed the Humber. I radioed ahead to RAF Cranwell and was given permission to land there. As I came in to land, I was aware of a lot of activity around one particular hangar. As soon as I got across to the Mess, I knew that something was going on. I could feel it and nobody would tell me what it was. As it happened, I shared a room with Flight Lieutenant Geoffrey Bone who was an engine installer engineer for Power Jets and one of the nicest men I ever met. It was the first time I had come across Power Jets but I soon knew quite a lot about it but I couldn't get a word out of him about what was going on at Cranwell.

    It was still raining the next morning and blowing a gale but when there was a lull in the weather, I was asked if I would take the Martlet up and check the flying conditions and the height of the cloud base. Mine was the only aircraft on the base that was ready to fly. In the early evening the Control Tower asked me to make another weather test. This showed a slight improvement with better visibility and the decision was made to make the test flight. People started to collect along the runway. There were about two hundred of us, a large group from Power Jets and about a hundred men from Cranwell who, like me, were curious to know what was happening. Then the hangar doors opened and we caught our first sight of E 28/39, a small, propellerless aeroplane with a tricycle undercarriage was pushed out. Gerry Sayer, Gloster's Chief Test Pilot was already in the cockpit and he taxied it, slowly at first but gathering speed, across to the runway. There were no official photographers, nobody from the ministry, just the few of us standing there about to witness one of the greatest occasions in the history of aviation. There had been nothing about the day to suggest that I was about to see the first flight of Britain's first jet aircraft, the Gloster E 28/39. But, even after it had landed, I wasn't really aware of how important that flight had been. It was only later that the full significance of the occasion really occurred to me.

Sub Lieutenant Eric Brown in his Martlet on May 14th 1941

It took off with a scream after a run of about 600 yards and, for a while, was lost in the clouds. It made a couple of turns before it landed 17 minutes later. It was the start of flight as we know it today. A time limit had evidently been set because only 50 gallons of fuel had been put in the tank so that the weight was kept down to give E 28/39 the best chance of lifting off.

I had noticed the short Wing Commander at the front of the spectators but I had no idea who he was until somebody told me that he was Frank Whittle. I was only a sub. Lieutenant so I didn't approach him. There wasn't a lot of exuberance but champagne was being passed round. It didn't reach me.

Sub Lieutenant Eric Brown

Extract from Frank Whittle's diary.
  'May 15th 1941
    First flight of E 28/39 this evening.

It wasn't that Frank Whittle was modest, he simply did not believe in wasting time or effort. Like all great thinkers, he was single minded. This engine had been dominating his life for thirteen years. His interests were science, engineering and flying. Anything else such as sport was a waste of time. He could not stand time wasters and officials from the Ministry were like red rags to a bull. But to his test pilots and those who worked for or with him, he was kindness itself. There is no doubt in my mind that Frank Whittle was a genius.

Eric Brown

Fourteen flights adding up to a total of ten hours of flying followed in the next two weeks without any need to lift the engine cover. During these weeks, the aircraft had reached a height of 25,000 feet and proved that approximately an hour's flight could be achieved on a tank full of fuel, 81 gallons. When the engine was stripped down, only the washers and rubber seals as well as a few nuts and bolts needed replacing.

Date or period (1)	Flying or Running Time		Total Flying or Running Time		Remarks (6)
	Hours (2)	Mins. (3)	Hours (4)	Mins. (5)	
Brought forward	—	—			
APR. 7-8. 1941	1	29			INITIAL TAXYING AT THE GLOSTER AIRCRAFT Co Ltd. A. Richards for I/c at the Gloster Aircraft Co Ltd CONTRACTORS TAXYING & FLIGHT TRIALS AT R.A.F. STATION CRANWELL.
14-5-1941		25	1	54	TAXYING ONLY
15-5-41		17		17	FIRST FLIGHT
16-5-41		24		41	FLIGHT AFTER ADJUSTING NOSEWHEEL JACK
oo		32	1	13	COOLING SYSTEM DRAINED & REFILLED WITH 70% WATER 30% GLYCOL.
Do		46	1	59	FLIGHT SATISFACTORY
17-5-41		34	2	33	DO.
oo		28	3	1	PT. U/C SHOCK ABSORBER REMOVED & REPLACED AFTER CHECKING PRESSURE. ELEVATOR CABLES ADJUSTED.
oo		49	3	50	NEW STBRD WHEEL FITTED
18-5-41		56	4	46	PT. SHOCKABSORBER CHANGED
Do		56	5	42	8" CORD TO TOP OF PT. AILERON.
21-5-41		15	5	57	8" CORD ADDED TO PT. AILERON. 6" CORD TO TOP & BOTTOM OF ELEVATORS. SUPPORT BRACKET FITT TO THROTTLE WARN. SWITCH. DOWN LOCK SWITCHES ADJ. PT. TYRE BURST WHEN LANDING. NEW PT. U/C WHEEL FITTED
21-5-41		12	6	9	DEMONSTRATION FLIGHT.
22-5-41		46	6	55	PT. AILERON — 1" CORD, PT. SIDE RUDDER + ½ CORD.
oo		42	7	37	TOP & BOTTOM OF ELEVATORS + 9" CORD.
27-5-41		26	8	3	AILERONS ADJ. TO GIVE ⅞ DROOP.
Carried forward	—	—	8	3	Above adj. & relevant flying times read. A. Richards for I/c A.I.D at The Gloster Aircraft Co. Ltd.

Log Book of E 28/39

Frank Whittle and Reactionaries watching the first flight.

The first jet flight completed – Frank Whittle congratulates Gerry Sayers

The aircraft was returned to the factory and another engine was fitted but there were several problems that had to be sorted out and it wasn't until later in 1942 that E 28/39 took to the air again watched by some visiting American guests. This was Gerry Sayer's last flight in the aircraft as he was killed a few weeks later when his Typhoon crashed into the sea. Fortunately, Michael Daunt, his assistant was involved with the project and was able to take over as the test pilot.

In March 1943, the second aircraft, fitted with a Rover W2B engine with 1,200 lb thrust joined the programme, while the first one was moved to RAE (Royal Aircraft Establishment) for RAF pilots to try out the new technology. The two aircraft continued with tests and in June 1943, John Grierson, wearing a specially designed pressure suit, took the second prototype to an altitude of 42,170 feet. He had inhaled pure oxygen for half an hour before taking off.

The two aircraft were retired in 1944 when the first British jet fighter, the Gloster Meteor, went into service with the RAF. The first jet engined aircraft to fly, the E 28/39, is on display at the Science Museum in London.

Frank Whittle was born at 72, Newcombe Road, a row of working class houses in Earlsdon, Coventry on June 1st 1907. His Grandparents and parents had worked in a Lancashire cotton mill, his father starting work at the age of ten and his mother at eleven. They were strict Wesleyans. Moses, Frank's father, was a skilful mechanic. He was always thinking of new ideas and inventions but did not have the knowledge or education to develop them. He and his wife did not want to spend their lives working twelve hours a day in a mill. They were determined to better themselves so, when they married, they moved to Ladywood, Coventry where Moses got a job in a small factory making machine tools. Frank was born at Ladywood, the eldest of three children. He experienced poverty and want from an early age. He remembered feeling shabby except on Sundays when the family wore their best clothes and attended the long Church services. After Church, his father would sit down with him and draw technical drawings that fascinated the young boy. He looked forward to these sessions with his father and, as he grew older, he started to add his own drawings and ideas.

His father always wanted to work for himself and, in 1916, he borrowed some money and bought the Leamington Valve and Piston Ring Company. It was a small workshop with a few lathes powered by a single cylinder gas engine. Frank would often help when they were busy. The firm prospered during the war years but, like many other small businesses of the time, this changed and his parents found it hard to survive. There was a time when they could not afford the rent for the house and had to live in the workshop. It was about this time that Frank won a scholarship which gave him the choice of ten pounds a year or a place at the local grammar school. There was no way that his parents could afford to buy him a uniform for the grammar school so he took the money and studied at Leamington College. Thus Frank had a working class background which he hated. He knew that people looked down on his family because they were poor and he was determined to escape from this image.

At this stage, he was a small, intelligent boy but he was already developing the character which would hold him in good stead as an adult. He could not be bothered with homework thinking that the time was better spent in the reference library reading up his favourite topics. He considered sport and physical exercise another waste of time. Anything to do with engineering, chemistry, mathematics or the sciences fascinated him. It was probably better that he did attend the College rather than the Grammar School because his teachers at the College realised that trying to get him to do anything that he didn't want to was a waste of time and allowed him to spend sports lessons in the library or one of the laboratories. It was in the reference library that he came across the steam turbine engine for the first time and learnt about its promise as a prime mover and, even then, wondered if it would be any use in aircraft. He became so confident about aeronautical engineering that he reckoned he could fly an aeroplane without having any lessons.

Frank was a schoolboy during the First World War and, like many other boys, he became fascinated with aircraft especially as one made a forced landing near him and his friends on Hearsall Common one day. He saw early warplanes being built at the Standard Works outside Coventry. This fascination stayed with him for the rest of his life and, by the time he was a teenager, he had decided that he wanted to fly and he wanted to join the Royal Flying Corps which became the Royal Air Force on April the first 1918.

During the First World War, the Royal Navy was growing concerned about German submarines in the North Sea and the movements of the Zeppelins which were flying over the Eastern Counties and bombing our towns. Navigation was an unknown science and the Zeppelins used the clock tower at Grimsby as their navigational point on the east coast, giving them easy access to the Humber and across northern England. The navy had ordered more airships and needed to establish stations from which airships and aircraft could fly over the North Sea. A naval pilot flew over East Anglia, searching for a site where the land was flat and not divided by deep dykes. Six sites in Lincolnshire were noted. Cranwell was one of them and the most suitable. The land was owned by the Bristol Estates and farmed by a Mr Usher Banks. A few days later, a Chief Petty Officer, eighteen ratings and a Foden truck arrived and started work on the new airfield. Before it was ready, the first aeroplane landed flown by Flight Lieutenant Maynard. Two days later, Air Commodore Sir Godfery Paine and his staff moved into the old farm house. Sir Godfery was a very energetic man. That night, the first airship flew over the site but it wasn't one of ours. It was a German Zeppelin.

We all ran for cover and sheltered in ditches or trenches. The Zeppelin made a dreadful noise but it didn't drop any bombs. It was night and so dark that the crew wouldn't have been able to see us anyway but we could see it alright with its huge outline against the night sky.

NK.

It came back three days later but, this time, the navy were ready for it and turned our guns on to it. One of the shells tore the envelope of the balloon but the Zeppelin escaped and made for home, dropping its bombs overboard as it went. Ten of the bombs were dropped over Rauceby. They didn't cause any harm. It was some time before another one visited the area.

Submarine Scout airship stationed at Cranwell

    I went to visit Cranwell with my aunt. She had known the family that used to farm there. We had never seen such a transformation in our lives. The woods and fields and muddy lane had all gone. Instead

there were roads and rows of huts. My aunt spoke to the sentry and he let us through to see what they had made of it. On one side of the road we could see aeroplanes landing and taking off and, over on our left, were more sheds, all sizes of sheds, some made of canvas, and three huge balloons tossing in the wind and there were four airships flying in the air above our heads at the same time. I had never seen anything so thrilling in my whole life.

M.Cant.

Fire engine stationed at Cranwell

Even before Frank Whittle arrived at RAF Cranwell in Lincolnshire, he demonstrated the skills that would, not many years later, enable him to overcome the huge weight of opposition facing him for the design and production of his revolutionary jet engine.

When he applied for an apprenticeship at the prestigious RAF Halton College as a small and frail 15 year old, he didn't let being turned down on medical grounds from stopping him applying again despite the fact that only one application a student was ever allowed. He simply forgot his first application, applied again and was accepted and became 364365 Apprentice Whittle F. – a fitter.

Frank demonstrated an incredible ingenuity although not always at the most appropriate times. It almost resulted in him failing his exams for a cadetship at Cranwell. In one question where he was asked to explain the system of a Rolls Royce engine, he described a completely different system which he considered to be superior believing the original question to be a waste of time.

Apprentices were paid five shillings a week and ten shillings a week when they became eighteen.

Frank as an apprentice with a model aeroplane he had designed and built

Mr H.A. Cox, the senior education officer of the Apprentice Wing was faced with the conundrum of how to prevent a student who was clearly so talented from being disqualified. His son tells the story of how his father spent hours juggling the marks to make sure that Whittle's paper was in the top six. Wing Commander Barton, another one of his lecturers, had also fought hard for him considering that he was a mathematical genius. He fought so hard that Trenchard, Marshal of the RAF said, "If you have made a mistake in this, Barton, I shall never forgive you."

The five top apprentices would qualify for a place as cadets. Frank Whittle was actually placed sixth but one of the boys failed his medical and Frank reported to RAF College, Cranwell as an officer cadet. He had not made his mark on the playing fields as many of the other students had done but his work in design and flight of model aeroplanes had shown his basic skills.

At first, he found life difficult as a cadet. In those days, people were very conscious of class. Bright, working class boys were expected to be apprenticed as befitted their status and Frank Whittle was a working class boy. The social gap was wide and Frank was not the sort of young man that would appeal to the more flamboyant, sports playing ex public school boys who provided the majority of the Cranwell cadets at that time.

Despite his humble beginnings, Frank Whittle was a good scholar.

It is important to realise that Whittle's world was more class based than our world is today. Birth and money still count in the social structure of today but they were immensely powerful in his time in determining the kind of education and the life chances available to him. Young working class people were particularly discriminated against. Bright, working class boys were expected to be apprenticed to a trade. After the First World War, the divisions widened. There was a massive distribution of wealth in the country, two thirds of which was in the hands of just one per cent of the population but new industrial practices and changing work patterns meant there was a need for more people to be trained and assume positions of responsibility.

Officer status was hard to come by for a working class boy. In the early days, commissions could be purchased although this was never a practice in the RAF. But something of the class divide lingered until well beyond the two World Wars.

Here was a young man who started life with few advantages beyond a loving family and a good brain. Having battled his way past social, academic and financial obstacles, he succeeded in creating something which changed the world. – Daily Mail.

He was one of the minority of great inventors to be reared in a working class background, haunted by the shadow of poverty, Frank said of himself that he was 'a street urchin on six days a week and a carefully dressed little boy on Sunday.'

Thus it was that Frank entered the RAF, not as an officer cadet but as 364365 Apprentice Whittle F. – a fitter.

He had done well as an apprentice, it was different as a cadet. Most of his contemporaries had been to public schools and were used to the customs and standard of living that was expected of him at the College. He was faced with white table cloths and a variety of cutlery at meal times whereas he had been used to putting his cutlery in his top pocket and queuing for his food. Fortunately a friendly waiter saw his dilemma and whispered the correct order of things to him. First termers had to wear suits and bowler hats until their uniforms were ready. He knew how much his parents had sacrificed to provide these for him but there was nothing he could do when other cadets took his bowler and used it as a football. There was no way he could replace it. It was not the only time that he felt out of place but he was determined not to let it upset him. He knew he had a chance in the

RAF that would allow him to fulfil his ambitions and he was going to achieve them. He never failed throughout his life to appreciate what the Air Force had done for him.

Whittle as a cadet

He did find it difficult at first to adapt to the different standard of living and understand the backgrounds of most of the cadets. Less than two percent of the apprentices who became cadets completed the course but Frank was determined to do so. To most of his fellow cadets, Frank was the first working class man that they had met on equal terms. He was not the sort of person who would appeal to the team spirited, flamboyant fraternity but he did not let their taunts worry him. His main ambition at that time was to fly and, as an officer cadet, this was his chance to learn.

Avro 504K

He flew solo in an Avro 504 K biplane in 1927 and graduated to Bristol Fighters.

Bristol Fighter

He loved flying but took far too many chances. He got into trouble for hedge hopping and low flying and, marked in his log book in red ink are warnings of over confidence. He earned a reputation for the risks he took. Although flying was an important part of his life, it was science - mathematical calculations, physics and the theory of flight in particular that fascinated him. Professor Sinnatt, his instructor at Cranwell, recognised his talent and encouraged him.

One of the requirements of the course was that students had to produce a thesis for graduation. Whittle wrote his thesis on the future of aircraft design.

In his thesis, he started by observing that the Air Ministry believed the gas turbine was impractical as an engine to power an aircraft. He set out his reasons and ideas to prove that it was practical.

I had come to the conclusion that if very high speeds were to be combined with long range, it would be necessary to fly at great height where the low air density would greatly reduce resistance in proportion to speed. The maximum speed for RAF fighters was 150mph and the ceiling was 20,000 feet. I wanted to fly at speeds of 500mph (800 km.ph) or more where the air was so thin that there would not be a big resistance at such a high speed. I thought this would only be possible with an entirely new kind of engine. It seemed unlikely to me that a piston engine and propeller combination would meet the high speed, high altitude aircraft I had in mind. I discussed the possibilities of rocket propulsion and of gas turbines driving propellers.

Avro 504Ns lined up at Cranwell

Whittle's thesis was called Future Developments in Aircraft Design and was a discussion of rocket propulsion and gas turbine driven propellers as alternatives to the conventional piston engines then available.

He described what we now call a motor-jet, a motor using a conventional piston engine to push compressed air into a combustion chamber whose exhaust would provide thrust, i.e. an after burner attached to an engine that turned a propeller. The idea had been known and discussed for some time but Whittle claimed that at higher altitudes, the lower pressure outside the aircraft would increase its efficiency. An aircraft on a long range flight would spend most of its time at a high altitude and, so, could perform better than the usual power plant. An example in his thesis states that if an aircraft flying at ground level reaches 60mph, using the same amount of thrust, it will travel at 300mph at an altitude of 35,000 feet.

He tackled the question of power in his thesis saying that normal aircraft of the time could not cope with high altitudes because they used piston engines (similar to those used in cars) which require a lot of air to function properly. The engine required a supercharger to function at high levels but the supercharger would use up far too much energy to make it practicable. Whittle then talked about creating a new engine.

I first started thinking about the gas turbine in my fourth term as a Flight Cadet at RAF Cranwell. We had to write a science thesis and I chose the future development of aircraft for my subject. I discussed the possibilities of jet propulsion and of gas turbines but it was not until eighteen months later when I was on an Instructors course at RAF Wittering, I conceived the idea of using a gas turbine for jet propulsion.

Whittle training as a pilot 1928

Even after his thesis had been submitted, Whittle continued to work on this idea but gave it up when he worked out that his engine would weigh as much as a conventional one. But then he thought that instead of using an internal combustion engine, a turbine could extract power from the exhaust that could power a compressor. The left over exhaust would power the aircraft.

Whittle sent this new idea up to the Air Ministry to see if they were interested in it. They turned to the only man they knew that had researched compressors and turbines, Dr A.A. Griffith. Griffith had already published a paper on compressors and turbines which he had studied at the RAE (Royal Aircraft Establishment) at Farnborough. Frank had described how the increased efficiency of these kinds of compressors and turbines would allow a jet engine to be produced but Griffith felt the idea was impractical. He thought that Whittle's design would not be suitable. He thought that compressors would be too large for aircraft use and that using a jet for direct power would be inefficient.

The main argument against the gas turbine was that maximum temperatures permissible with the available materials or likely to be available would not be great enough to allow a reasonable margin of useful work.

If the RAF had taken up Whittle's idea, the jet engine would have become their property. As it was, he retained his own rights.

In many ways, Frank had joined the RAF at a most exciting time. He had seen aircraft that had been used during the First World War being adapted for civilian flights. He had seen ideas of design and engines being developed. It wasn't only in aircraft but in every aspect of post war Britain but it was aircraft that fascinated Frank. There was a feeling of challenge and adventure about flying that made him determined about his own future. At this time, Cranwell boasted the longest runway in the world and some of the challengers

flew from the station. In 1927, Flight Lieutenants C.R. Carr and L.E.M. Gillman attempted a non stop flight to India and in April 1929 Squadron Leader A.G. Jones-Williams and Flight Lieutenant N.H. Jenkins made a non stop flight to Karachi, 4,130 miles in 50 hours, a world record.

In 1927 Lindbergh flew non stop from New York to Paris, the same year that the RAF recaptured the Schneider trophy for Britain. Experiments with metal frames for aircraft were being conducted.

Flt Lts Carr and Gillman

The clever part of Whittle's reasoning was that the jet engine could be powerful enough to propel an aircraft and he was also able to complete the complicated calculations that would prove this possible. At this stage though, he was thinking of the jet engine as a means of turning the propellers but these were only ideas. He was already thinking about aircraft that could fly higher and faster and about the ways this could be made to happen.

The Prize Winners – July 1928 Whittle is standing in the centre, back row

Passing out parade 1928 Whittle is 3rd from left on back row

Whittle passed out from Cranwell College in July 1928. He was posted firstly to Hornchurch, a fighter squadron flying Siskins and then to Wittering for a flying instructor's course.

Crazy flying at the RAF Pageant, Hendon, with Whittle (from FTS at Digby, ex-No 111 Fighter Squadron) flying one of the 504Ns.

It was while he was there that he was selected to fly at the RAF Hendon Air show with Flying Officer G. Campbell in the crazy flying display. Whittle crashed two of the planes in practice and a furious Flight Commander asked him why he didn't take all his planes and burn them. It would have been quicker. Complaints were made to the police about his low flying. There was a bit of the daredevil in Whittle. He took chances that other pilots would not attempt but he knew the planes he flew and their limitations. His flying displays became popular with crowds that attended the air shows of the day. He gave solo displays at the Hendon Air show on several occasions.

But, even while he was flying, he was still thinking of ways of developing his jet engine. It was while he was at Wittering that he suggested that the turbine could produce a propelling jet rather than one that drove a propeller. The Air ministry heard about his ideas and knew that he was a clever boy but showed no interest in them.

There was another flying instructor at Wittering who listened to Whittle and questioned him about his ideas. Flying Officer Pat (Johnny) Johnson was impressed. He arranged an interview with the Commandant. Whittle received a call from the Ministry inviting him to meet Dr A.A. Griffiths at the Ministry's laboratories in South Kensington. It was not a happy meeting. Griffiths questioned his calculations and reported that there was nothing in Whittle's ideas and his scheme was impractical. Nevertheless, Whittle did take out a patent for the engine on Johnny Johnson's recommendation.

I applied for a patent for the gas turbine engine concept, a reaction motor suitable for aircraft propulsion. This was granted in April 1931 but, unfortunately, the idea continued to be ignored by the Air Ministry.

However, Frank Whittle was not a man to compromise or be concerned with setbacks.

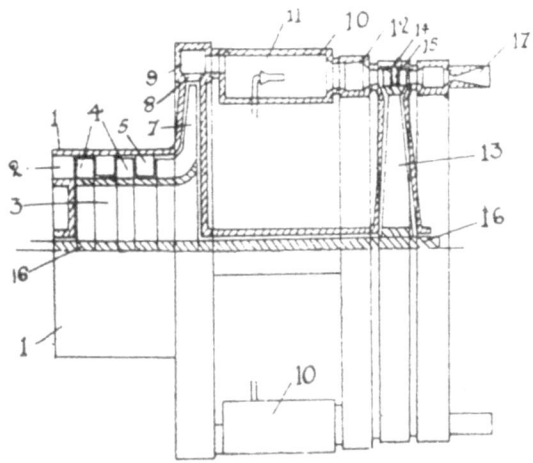

Drawing from the registered patent

Wedding day

Frank married his childhood sweetheart in 1930 and, because he was so young, he had to get special permission from the Commanding Officer. He now had serious problems. It was not easy for two of them to survive on a young officer's pay and he was not old enough to receive a marriage allowance.

His parents did not attend the wedding, probably thinking that he was in no position to support a wife, especially one that came from a family that was more prosperous than they were. It took several years before they were reconciled.

He was transferred to the Marine Aircraft Establishment at RAF Felixstowe in 1931 as a test pilot where he worked on the floating and sinking times of various sea planes. He had many exciting times here although the one that stayed in his memory was when he was catapulted from the Ark Royal. His passenger, Flight Lieutenant Kirk, lost his grip in the rear cockpit and bounced up into the air. Fortunately, he managed to catch hold of the fin and held on but Whittle had difficulty in landing the plane and only just missed hitting a German liner.

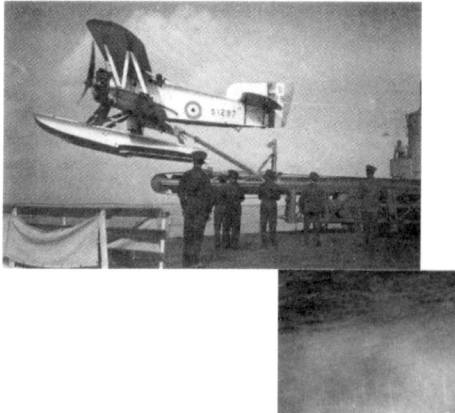

Later that year he moved to RAF Digby as an instructor for No. 2 Flying Training School.

All officers holding permanent commissions at that time were expected to undertake specialist studies and, to this end, Frank Whittle went to RAF Henlow,

He achieved 98% in all subjects at the Officer's School of Engineering in 1932. This gave him the confidence to ask to be referred to Cambridge University to read Mechanical Sciences. By 1934, the RAF was prepared to sponsor the idea for a jet engine and, as a mature student, he was sent to Cambridge starting at Peterhouse in 1934. He completed his degree in the Mechanical Sciences Tripos with first class honours in only two years instead of the usual three. His tutor at Peterhouse College was Sir Melvill Jones, Head of the department of Aeronautical Engineering.

This was when Whittle almost gave up his ideas of developing the jet engine. His first son had been born and he had bills to pay. He was finding it difficult to manage on his RAF pay.

Developing an engine needed money and Frank could not even afford to sustain his patent because of lack of funds. It was while he was at Cambridge that the patent on his invention ran out. He did not have a hope of paying the £5 that was needed to renew it especially as he was already having doubts that it would ever be fully developed. So his ideas and calculations were released to the public and became known throughout the world. In fact, the plans of his proposed engine were written up in a German newspaper within days of the patent running out.

The Air Ministry had taken Dr A.A. Griffith's advice that his turbojet concept had insufficient merit and was not worth further attention. Whittle knew what his turbojet could achieve. He had checked and rechecked his mathematical calculations but there was nowhere and nobody else that he could approach to help him make his invention a reality. It seemed that everywhere he looked for help he was being met with a brick wall. It looked like the end of his hopes and he started to turn his thoughts towards his career in the

RAF. The likelihood was that he would be posted abroad and if that happened, he wouldn't have been able to continue with the work on the turbojet.

It was about this time that Roy Lubbock, his professor at Cambridge, contacted the Air Ministry and suggested that they gave Whittle a research fellowship for a further year. They agreed and he was able to concentrate on his turbojet project for another year.

It was also at this time that he received a letter from his room mate at Cranwell, Rolf Dudley Williams. Although Whittle had seemed the odd one out when he first became a Cadet at Cranwell, he had earned the respect of the other cadets and Rolf, in particular, had always shown an interest in his work and ideas. In his letter, he said that he had met a man who was interested in Whittle's idea of a jet engine and would like to meet him. He suggested a meeting.

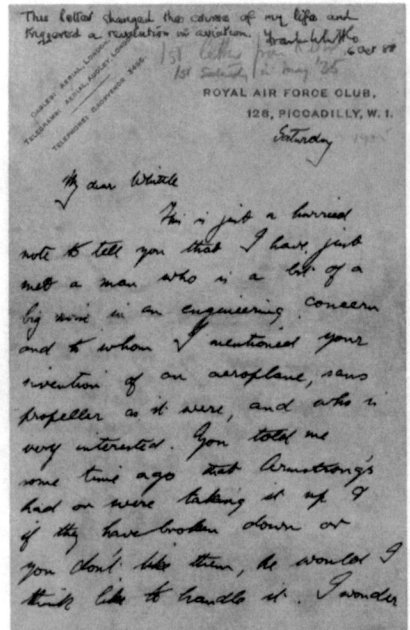
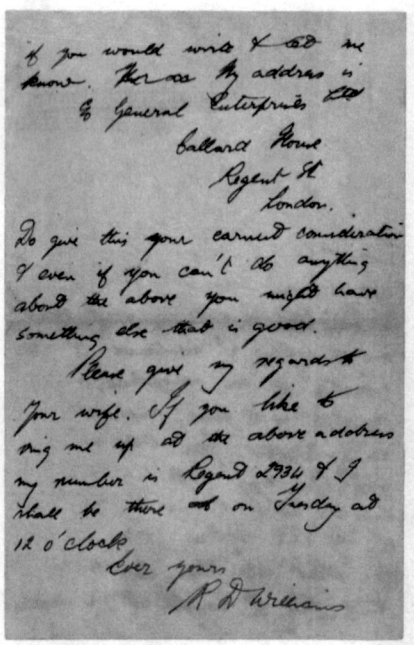

Whittle wrote: This letter changed my life and triggered a revolution in aviation (see top left hand of letter)

> *Just a hurried note to tell you that I have just met a man who is a bit of a big noise in an engineering concern and to whom I mentioned your invention of an aeroplane, sans propeller as it were, who is very interested – Do give this your earnest consideration and even if you can't you might have something else that is good……………*

Whittle read the letter and pushed it in his pocket and promptly forgot about it. He had received so many similar letters, all of which had ended in disappointment. Finding the letter in his pocket some time later, he looked at it and decided that he had nothing to lose and met Williams and his friend Tinling in Cambridge. After some discussion, they offered to raise enough money to develop the engine. From that moment, things began to move. Negotiations started in 1935 and an agreement was reached in early November with the creation of Power Jets Ltd. The patent had been re-registered and, because Frank Whittle was in the RAF, the patent application was subject to a formal agreement with the Air Ministry. Dudley Williams and Tinling planned to raise £50,000, (equivalent to £2,000,000 in today's terms), a huge sum in those days. A firm of bankers, Falk and Partners retained Bramson, a well known pilot and an engineer to write a report on the project. He was enthusiastic and another step forward was made with the formation of Power Jets Ltd. Whittle, Tinling and Williams were to hold a 49% share in the company. Although he was allotted shares in the company, Whittle had to hand over the patent rights to Power Jets. Power jets Ltd was to develop Whittle's jet engine. The company was incorporated in March 1936.

Lancelot Law Whyte, a member of the bank, was appointed to manage the money for the bank because of his scientific interests. When he was told that a young flight lieutenant had invented a new aero engine, he was reluctant to meet him but they did meet and he was completely won over saying that he was happy to meet a man who maintained his own high standards. Whittle had imagination, ability, enthusiasm, respect for science and he had thought of this stunningly simple idea, a 2,000 hp engine with a single moving part. He told his wife that he had met one of the greatest inventive engineers of their time.

Receiving his degree at Peterhouse College, Cambridge

The RAF put Whittle on to the Special Duties list which enabled him to have a dual role. He acted as Honorary Chief Engineer for Power Jets Ltd as well as being a serving officer.

Whittle hadn't waited for the agreement to be finalised. He had waited so long for this chance and he was impatient to get started. They had agreed that they would place a contract for an experimental engine to be built and Whittle approached B.T.H. (British Thomson Houston) of Rugby to make the necessary drawings to his own specifications. They were to be of an engine to power a small plane and were to consist of a single centrifugal compressor driven by a single stage turbine at up to 17,750 rpm. This was far in advance of anything that had already been proposed. Work started in January but Whittle was so disappointed in the drawings the firm produced, he revised them himself. Then BTH started work on the detailed drawings and, by the end of 1936, the design work had been finished.

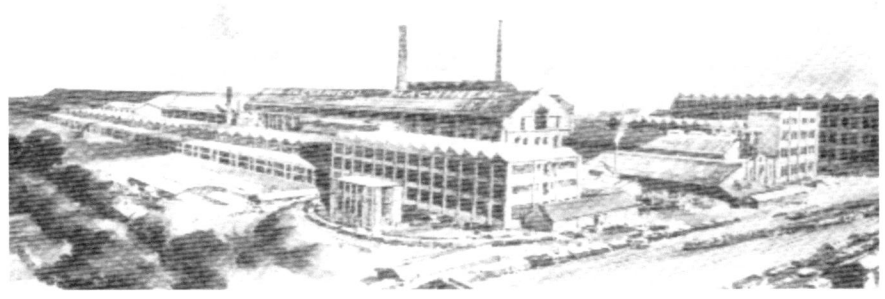

BTH factory

Funding the development of his engine became a problem from the start. Potential investors were reluctant to back it because it did not have the full support of the RAF and they couldn't understand why it didn't.

But there were others that did support him. Henry Tizard, Rector of Imperial College, London and Chairman of the Aeronautical Research Committee, sent Griffith details of Whittle's engine and asked him to look at them again. Tizard had been arguing for an aircraft that could achieve the maximum excess speed over the bomber. "What I want is an engine which gives terrific power for its size and weight." Whittle's engine obviously fell into that category.

By this time, Griffith had started working on his own design. He returned a more positive report on the engine than he had done before but was still critical and completely ignored the fact that its performance at high speed and high altitude was the most important aspect. Despite all the problems, Power Jets completed the WU which ran successfully on April 12th, 1937. Tizard managed now to persuade the Air Ministry to fund further development with a grant of £6,000 to develop a version that would fly although it was a year before the money appeared.

Power Jets had one employee, Victor Crompton, but they had arranged with BTH that they could borrow workers if and when they were needed and there were times when they did need them, even having to call in the night watchman to give a hand from time to time. By the end of 1940, the company had grown to 134 employees.

BTH allowed Power Jets to use the area outside the firm's turbine factory to carry out testing. It meant they had to work outside but it was a covered area because there were offices above the site.

The Workshop (Photo: courtesy of Lutterworth Museum)

They weren't protected from the weather though. Neither were the staff in the offices protected from the noise and fumes. They complained that the floor would sometimes shake so much that it lifted the lino from the floor and papers were blown across the room. It reached the stage where the women staff took shelter in the toilets when the engine was started up.

Studying the drawings(Photo: courtesy of Lutterworth Museum)

Whittle was working on the massive WU engine. Things changed when the first test run of this prototype engine took place in 1937. It was not fastened to the ground. It started alright. The trouble came when they tried to stop it and there was a sudden acceleration from 2,500 rpm to 8,000 rpm. Fuel had dropped on the ground and formed a pool in the bottom of the conche shell combustion chamber and the engine did not stop accelerating until all the fuel on the ground had been used up. Fuel had also dropped on the surrounding area. Suddenly the escaping fuel burst into flames and the area filled with smoke. The fitters all took flight, Crompton in the lead, something that Whittle teased him about for the rest of his life. Whittle himself didn't move. He was intent on watching the dials, searching for the figures he had waited so long to see.

Alterations were made and the second test run took place the next day. Not only did the engine run away again but it was surrounded by a ring of fire and, once again, the men took flight and BTH decided that Power Jets would have to test their engine elsewhere. They offered the disused foundry at the Ladywood works in Lutterworth. Power Jets moved there on the 4th of March 1938. Further buildings were added as they were needed.

A fuel consumption test at Lutterworth (Photo: courtesy of Lutterworth Museum)

One of the first things Whittle did when they moved was to get a guard dog from Battersea Dogs' Home as the site was isolated and he obviously thought a guard dog would help protect the place. The dog didn't fully understand its role and, at the first noise, it was off and the office boy spent a large part of his day searching for it. Power Jets Ltd appointed their first apprentice draughtsman, Roy Malcolm Green, in August 1941. One of his duties was to help find the dog.

Another thing Whittle did was to employ a secretary, Mary Phillips. Until then, he and Crompton had been typing up the letters and reports between them and neither of them showed any particular ability with a type-writer.

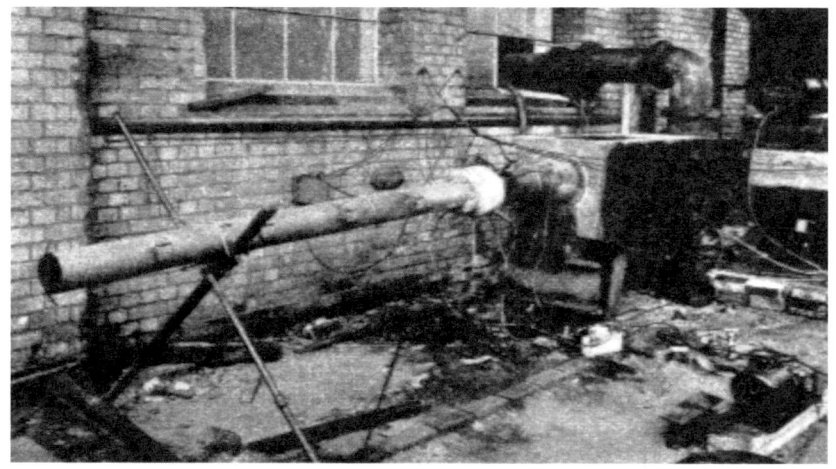

The first combustion chamber (Photo: courtesy of Lutterworth Museum)

Frank Whittle was an RAF Officer and, officially, he was only spending six hours a week on his engine but in the summer of 1937 he was transferred to the special duties list to work full time on the project and promoted to Squadron Leader.

Testing the W2-700 engine (Photo: courtesy of Lutterworth Museum)

A turbine is an important part of the engine. It is a device for rotating a shaft with a series of blades arranged radially round it. These are fitted at an angle so that a gas or liquid flowing over it will cause the shaft and blades to rotate.

Whittle's engine consisted of four basic parts, a compressor, a combustion chamber, a turbine and a propelling nozzle. Air is drawn into the compressor via the air intake. Fuel is mixed with air and burned in the combustion chamber. The hot gas drives the turbine and the exhaust leaves the engine via the nozzle. The turbine which is connected to the compressor provides the power to compress the air and the gas leaving the nozzle provides the thrust to propel the aircraft forward.

In June 1939, David Pye, the director of Scientific Research saw a twenty minute test run of the WU at speeds of up to 16,000rpm. In January, 1940, Air Vice Marshal Tedder also saw a test run and said that he felt he was in the presence of a 'real war winner'. The WU was the model for the geometrically similar unit, the W1 which was built from entirely new components and powered the E 28/39.

Turbines get very hot. In the combustion chamber of a typical commercial jet, gases can reach 2,000 degrees Celsius and the gases will not decrease in temperature before reaching the turbine.

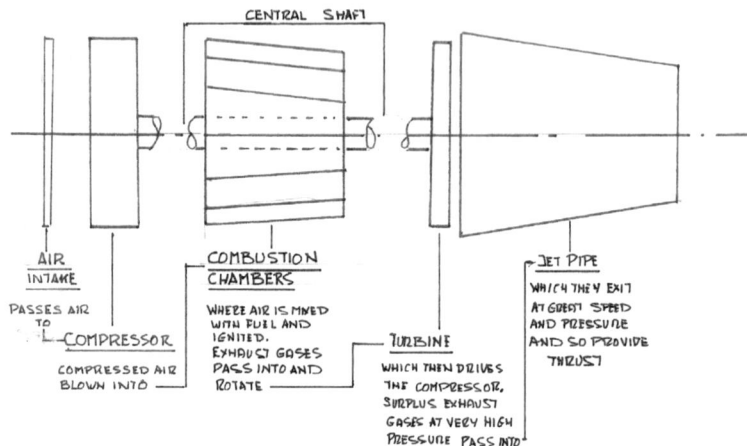

One of the problems that Frank Whittle encountered was finding suitable materials that would withstand the extreme heat that his jet engine would produce, particularly the blades. It was by pure chance that he met Mr Laidlaw from Edinburgh, a director of Laidlaw, Drew and Company. He advised Whittle on the type of material he could use for the blades as well as for other parts of the engine.

Frank Whittle's energy, enthusiasm and attention to detail was formidable. He would travel to Edinburgh to visit Laidlaw, then return to Sheffield to see how the forging of the turbine wheels was proceeding and then on to Slough to see the compressor being forged and all the time, he was working out what next step had to be made and was worried that there would not be enough financial support to complete the project but, despite all his worries, the jet engine was beginning to emerge.

The site at Lutterworth wasn't ideal. Whittle's office overlooked the railway line and he swore that the engine drivers waited until they were in position outside his window before they let off steam. The site wasn't as secure as he thought it should have been and he took to sleeping on a camp bed in his office. He wasn't worried about bombs dropping but he didn't want a German spy descending by parachute and stealing his drawings. Local people began to be suspicious about what was going on at the works and the rumour spread round the town that they were working on a new kind of flame thrower. Then a more serious rumour went round that they were making bombs for the IRA. That brought the local policeman to investigate. Crompton met him and told him as much as he could about what they were doing there and showed him round. Although he looked under the tables and in all the corners, he didn't seem any the wiser when he left.

One of the most amazing things about the whole story is that the secret of the development of the first jet engine was so well kept. Frank Whittle called his team of workers the Reactionaries. They were all sworn to secrecy and were all aware of how important the project was. It was Whittle himself who found it difficult to keep everything he was doing to himself. He had always discussed everything with his wife. Now he was first and foremost an RAF officer and the engine he was working on was top secret. He discussed it with nobody, especially not his wife. It was the first time they had kept anything from each other and they both found it difficult and Whittle felt the strain of the situation. He also developed a feeling of guilt that he was not actively fighting the Germans as the other pilots with whom he had trained were doing.

The period of the Second World War was not an easy time for Frank Whittle. As an above average pilot and flying instructor, he nevertheless had to sit back and watch as his time was spent on engine development while his colleagues were flying long sorties against the enemy. All around him, men he had known and valued were being killed, injured or being taken prisoner while he had what appeared to be a comfortable office bound job – but a vital one and one that was definitely secret.

Whittle was very relieved when his office was moved to Brownsover Hall because space was at a premium at Ladywood, so much so that he often found it difficult to get down the stairs because people were sitting on them working.

Working at Brownsover Hall

Whittle was not a business man. He did not understand finance and was worried that there would not be enough money to complete the engine. He was very careful with every tool. Materials and parts had to be used time and time again. Nothing was wasted.

Whittle never did anything without detailed, logical thought and calculations. He had an unrivalled grasp of the fundamentals of thermodynamics and aerodynamics.

"As I came to know him and his work better, I realised he had laid down the performance of jet engines with the precision of Newton."

Whittle accurately predicted what a jet engine would do before he ever made one. Others were also working on similar engines, most of whom intended to retain propellers and simply replace the piston engine by the gas turbine. Whittle set about designing a compressor when he realised that one had never been designed with the size and performance that he wanted.

As the engine was developed, more and more visitors came to the site to see what they were doing. Air Chief Marshal, Sir Hugh Dowding, Commander in Chief of Fighter Command was one of them. It was a visit that Frank Whittle never forgot. Whittle took him round the outside of the building. Sir Hugh approached a nozzle that was protruding from the wall. Whittle explained that he should not go near it but the Air Chief Marshal misunderstood and walked right up to it. At that moment there was a roar and he was hit by a huge current of air which blew his coat open, his hat high into the air and himself staggering across the concrete.

On the 6th of May, 1938, Whittle's engine was run for one hour and forty five minutes. Whittle was starting to see the success for which he had craved for so long. This was the first major step towards May 15th, 1941. After this, Power Jets started to look for an aeroplane for their engine. It so happened that Glosters were looking for an engine to power one of their aircraft. It couldn't have been better and they adapted their aircraft to meet Power Jets requirements. They called it E (Experimental) 28/39 – the Air

Ministry's 28th order in 1939. The first site where the tests took place is now the Gloucester Trading Estate. Its outline can still be seen clearly today from the air.

George Carter, Gloster's chief designer worked closely with Frank Whittle over the design of the E 28/39 and planned a low winged aircraft. The jet intake was in the nose and the exhaust was beneath the tail. The Air Ministry signed the contract for two of these aircraft in 1940 and, at last, Whittle could see his ideas coming to fruition after so many disappointments and setbacks. It was the first of these two aeroplanes that was completed in April 1941 and delivered to Hucclecote for ground testing on the 7th of that month.

I remember Gloster Engineering had a factory at Bentham, a small place about a mile from Brockworth where I lived. This must have been where the E 28/39 was built. There were all kinds of rumours going the rounds about what was happening there and then, one day, we saw this machine being towed up the road and that was that.   *A.L.*

The Gloucestershire Aircraft Company was founded in 1917 in Cheltenham during the First World War. They built the Nighthawk, a bi-plane fighter for use in the war and the Gloster Grebe that was used by the RAF in the 1920s as was the Gladiator, a good aircraft to fly but no match for the new breed of aeroplanes in use in the Second World War. They changed their name to Gloster in 1926 because so few customers from abroad were able to pronounce the name correctly. They were taken over by Hawkers in 1934 but still continued to use their original name for aircraft production. The Gloster factory then started producing the Hawker Hurricanes and Typhoons. During the Second World War, they developed a production line that could produce fifty Hurricanes a day.

The Germans seemed to know that something was going on near Gloucester because we had a lot of raids and bombs were dropped

on the area around the airfield. As the war progressed, our nights were often long, disturbed ones of anti-aircraft fire as bombers flew overhead. In the day time, we were aware when a raid was likely to take place when the barrage balloons went up around Brockworth where the Gloster Aircraft factory was based. One day, we all had to get off the bus and go into the air raid shelter until the all clear went.
Elsie B.

The Air Ministry specification and order to Glosters for the E 28/39 were signed by Roderick Hill on the 21st of January, 1940.

The order states that the maximum speed at sea level would not be less than 380 miles per hour and the rate of climb from sea level would not be less than 4,000 feet per minute. Armament was to be four Browning machine guns or cine camera guns and 2,000 rounds of ammunition. A reflective gun site was to be designed. Night flying equipment was not required. Total fuel to be 80 gallons and it was not to be starved of fuel if the aircraft was inverted. The aircraft was to be powered by a Whittle jet propulsion engine to be installed to the satisfaction of Power Jets Ltd.

Gloster E28/39 first prototype

A GLOSTER AIRCRAFT CO. LTD.

SECRET

TEST FLIGHT REPORT No.: 1

PILOT P.E.G.Sayer.

Type of Test : 1st Flight. General experience of the type.
Date and Time of Start 15.5.41.   1940 hrs.   Duration 17 mins.

AIRCRAFT: Type and No. E.28/39. W.4041.
Type of Undercarriage Dowty nose wheel type. All retractable.
Other Features Main wheel lever suspension type. Nose wheel strut type.

AIRSCREW: Type and No. No airscrew fitted with this method of propulsion.
Dia. :
Pitch Setting Fine   Coarse
Ground Clearance Flying Position   Tail on Ground

ENGINE: Type and No. Whittle Supercharger Type W.1.
Reduction Gear
R.P.M. O.G. Fine Pitch 16500 Take-off.   Coarse Pitch
Boost O.G.
Type of Air Intake
Radiator Stbd radiator blanked off. Port radiator in circuit.
Other Features

WEIGHTS CARRIED:
Fuel Paraffin 50 galls.   Oil 1 gall.
Cooling Liquid 3.5 galls water.
Total Weight 3441 lb. estimated from Two C.G.
C.G. Position .284 A.M.C. U/C Down. .297 A.M.C. U/C Up calculated from
Loading Sht. No. 142   Date 7.5.41.   (Tare C.G.

REMARKS:
Exhaust System
Cooling System   Nose wheel leg total travel 12" as against 10" on
Oil System   original nose wheel leg fitted for taxying trials at
Guns and Mountings Brockworth. Static travel 6" instead of 7" on the first leg.
Bombs and Racks   Nose wheel strut pressure reduced from 140 lbsq.in. to
Sights   115 lbsq.in, Tyre pressure reduced from 35 lbsq.in. to
Nav. and Ident. Lamps 80 lbsq.in.
Aerial   Steering on nose wheel 11° either side of the centre line
Fairing   Brakes on all three wheels.
Type of Cockpit Heating
Pilot Position & Type

TEST INSTRUMENTS:
Ican. Altimeter No. :   Calibrated
A.S.I. Instrument No. :
R.P.M.
Boost Gauge
Air Temp.

Signature of Pilot Sayer.

Test Flight report of the first flight of the E 28/39

Obviously the Ministry were aware of the potential of Frank Whittle's jet engine because the order was followed by another on the 14th of November, 1940 signed by H. Grinstead of the Ministry of Aircraft Development Department. The specification number for this order was F9/40. This twin engined fighter was to be designed to accommodate two W2B engines, 4x20mm guns and accessories, 600 rounds of ammunition and the maximum speed at 30,000 feet was to be not less than 430 miles per hour. This was to become the first operational jet fighter of WW2

Gloster Meteor III

Whittle had worked on the problems of turning the WU into a flyable design but Rover was unable to deliver it before Glosters experimental air-frame was ready so he made up an engine which he built up from different test parts. He called this engine WIX. It ran for the first time in December 1940. It also powered the Gloster E 28/39 for taxi testing when it made its first lift into the air for a few seconds on April 7th ,1941. With the taxi testing satisfactorily completed, the aircraft was fitted with a new turbojet which gave 3.8 kn (850 lbs) of thrust.

At this time, Rovers were responsible for the manufacture of the engine. Tinling's wife had known the wife of the managing director of the firm and so the introduction had been made but Whittle had been disappointed with them on a number of occasions and relations had become strained. It was not only that they had difficulty in meeting dead lines, they tended to alter details to suit their own ideas rather than adhere to the clear instructions that Whittle had given them.

Another visitor who had visited the Lutterworth site was Dr Stanley Hooker. He was a young engineer at Rolls Royce when he visited Ladywood.

Picture left: Whittle and Dr Stanley Hooker became good friends.

He found it difficult to believe that Whittle had achieved so much with such poor facilities, small number of staff and the minimum of financial help. He was impressed with what he saw but when he converted thrust into horsepower, he immediately realised the engine's potential. He went and saw Lord Hives, the head of Rolls Royce and told him that he should go and see what Power Jets were doing. Lord Hives was sceptical and wanted to know exactly what the engine could do and was told it gave 800lb of thrust. Lord Hives was not impressed saying that the thrust would not blow the skin off a rice pudding. When he was told that the Merlin engine in a Spitfire which flew at 300 mph gave 840 lbs, he immediately arranged to go to Lutterworth the following weekend.

It was the meeting that was to change the speed with which the work on the jet proceeded and gave Rolls Royce the lead in the field of aviation gas turbines.

Whittle showed the two men round and, when Lord Hives asked where the engines were and what was causing the delay, Whittle told him that he had difficulty in getting certain components made. Lord Hives told him to send the drawings to Derby and he would have them made up. There was no mention of payment and none was ever asked. Turbine blades, gear cases, etc were made at Derby and Dr Hooker was asked to keep an eye on what was happening at Lutterworth and keep Lord Hives informed.

Rolls Royce started back in 1884 with Henry Royce's electrical and mechanical business which built a motor car in 1904. In May that year Royce met a quality London car salesman named Charlie Rolls. An agreement was made that Henry would make the car to be exclusively sold by Charlie and would bear the name Rolls Royce. They started their journey to the top of the aeronautical industry back in 1914 when Royce designed the Eagle, his first aero engine. This engine powered the first direct transatlantic flight and the first flight from England to Australia. Subsequently Rolls Royce developed an engine that broke the air speed record of over 400mph in 1931.

Due to the critical decision to take responsibility for the production of Whittles engine Rolls Royce started a 'catch up' programme for aero gas turbines. This basically meant that Rolls Royce was placed at the forefront of gas turbine technology. Early problems with the RB211 engine meant Rolls Royce was taken over by the state and the car part of the company was separated entirely. By 1987 Rolls Royce returned to the private sector and became the only company in Britain to provide power for the air, sea and land. Rolls Royce is one of the biggest aeronautics company in the world providing over 54,000 gas turbines for the sea the land and the air. The company powers 500 airlines; 4,000 corporate, utility aircraft and helicopter operators. Rolls Royce also powers approximately 25% of the world military fleet.

Using compressor knowledge built upon many years of supercharger development, Rolls Royce set to work to gain a better understanding of the new jet technology with which it too had experimented under Dr A A Griffith in 1939.

It has often been speculated that had the vast resources of Rolls Royce been engaged with Whittle much sooner, then the jet would have been developed much earlier in the war. However, it must be borne in mind that Rolls Royce was operating at full capacity producing and developing the Merlin piston engine in great numbers at this time. There was little room for development of an entirely new form of propulsion.

The Whittle/Rover W.2B design was renamed the Welland. It was to become the custom to name Rolls Royce jet engines after British rivers, just as the piston aero engines had been named after birds of prey. The Welland first flew in a Gloster Meteor from the Rolls Royce Flight Test Facility at Hucknall in November 1943. Power Jets were working on the W.2/500 and W.2/700 and the Rolls Royce Derwent replaced the Welland. The increased thrust and improved reliability of these engines transformed the Meteor's performance, and it was to be the Derwent that would power the production Meteor. Even though Meteors were front-line jet fighters, few were ever to cross the Channel to operate in liberated airspace. This was to prevent them falling into enemy hands.

The Welland (Rolls Royce Heritage Trust)

During this period, other firms were also developing gas turbines and worked under the direction of the Gas Turbine Collaboration Committee and the Air Ministry. Firms such as Metropolitan Vickers, BTH, Armstrong Siddeley, Bristol, Napier and De Havilland contributed to the effort of turning the jet into an operational reality. In the course of time, most would merge in one form or another to become part of Rolls Royce.

An experimental derivative of the Derwent, the Trent, first flew in a Meteor in September 1945 and was the world's first turbo-propeller gas turbine aero engine. It provided valuable data for the design of later turboprop engines, such as the Clyde, Dart and Tyne.

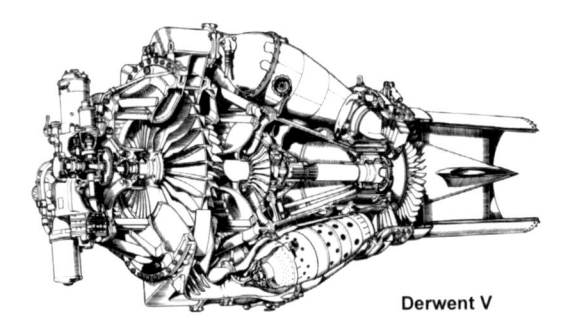

Derwent Cutaway (The Rolls Royce Heritage Trust)

Derwent production continued after the war and so too did the Rolls Royce Nene, at the time the most powerful engine in the world. Nenes were manufactured under licence in Canada, USA, Australia and France. It was also manufactured without licence in the Soviet Union and China and, as a result, the Nene saw combat in aircraft on both sides during the Korean war.

It was clear that the jet engine on civil aircraft would revolutionise air travel. Britain's first jet airliner, the De Havilland Comet was originally powered by DH Ghost engines but later marks used the Rolls Royce Avon, described later.

The threat of the Cold War meant that more jet aircraft projects were being launched and after the breaking of the "sound barrier" in

1947, supersonic flight heralded a new chapter in engine development.

The Avon (The Rolls Royce Heritage Trust)

The Avon was Rolls Royce's first axial turbojet, so called because it featured an axial flow compressor as opposed to the centrifugal compressors that R-R had previously used. The Avon flew in aircraft such as Canberra, Javelin, Sea Vixen, Hunter and, of course, the supersonic Lightning interceptor. The Avon also went on to see civilian use on the Comet and Sud-Aviation Caravelle. The Avon was converted for industrial power generation, gas pumping and marine propulsion. The Avon remained in RAF service in the Canberra until 28 July 2006, 57 years from the first Canberra flight. The axial flow compressor could develop much higher pressures in the compressor. But with higher pressures came higher operating temperatures and soon the limits of conventional materials were reached. High temperature steels and nickel based alloys were developed to improve temperature capability.

By the early 1950s the understanding of jet engine performance was becoming ever greater. It was no longer acceptable to pursue greater power regardless of efficiency. A new development came with the advent of the bypass turbofan. The Conway was the first engine to use a proportion of the cold inlet air stream to provide thrust. This reduces the noise and fuel consumption of the engine. The Conway was to become the power plant used in the Handley

Page Victor V-bomber. It was used on both the Vickers VC-10 and Boeing 707 airliners.

The 1960s and 70s saw a dramatic reduction in military and civil aircraft projects. One notable survivor was the Pegasus vectored thrust engine. The Pegasus, of course, is the engine for the Harrier "Jump Jet", the world's first vertical take-off and landing fighter and ground attack aircraft. The aircraft remains in service with the USMC, and the Thai, Spanish, Indian and Italian navies.

Pegasus VSTOL engine (The Rolls Royce Heritage Trust)

In 1969, the world's first supersonic airliner took to the air for the first time. Concorde was the result of Anglo-French collaboration and was expected to revolutionise modern air travel. However, environmental opposition about engine noise and sonic booms from many groups around the world, coupled with the oil crisis in the early seventies resulted in the only firm orders coming from the national airlines of Britain and France. In all 13 production aircraft were built powered by the Rolls Royce Olympus 593 engine, the only engines on a civil aircraft to use reheat. The last Concorde flight took place on 23 November 2003 ending the supersonic passenger jet era.

As the sixties drew to a close, Rolls Royce launched a three-shaft, high bypass ratio turbofan with revolutionary lightweight carbon fibre fan blades, the RB211. Technical difficulties with the new fan blade material led to a redesign of the fan which delayed the engines for the new Lockheed L1011 Tristar wide body airliner. This coupled with escalating costs led to Rolls Royce being put in the unfortunate position of going into receivership in February 1971. Thanks to the efforts of the employees and the receiver himself, Rolls Royce (1971) Limited emerged from the proceedings with the RB211 programme intact. The RB211-22B and -524 went on to become a success on the Tristar, Boeing 747 and, with the smaller RB211-535 version, on the Boeing 757.

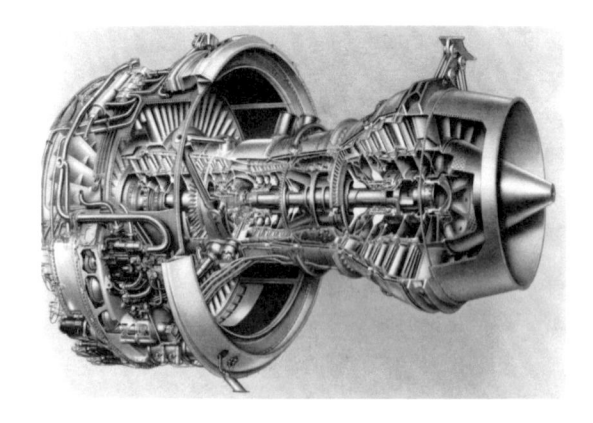

RB211 cutaway (The Rolls Royce Heritage Trust)

When the company was privatised in 1987, the RB211 was the core of the civil engine business for Rolls Royce plc. The RB211 three-shaft family was further developed into the highly successful Trent family of engines used on airliners today, such as the Boeing 787 and the Airbus A380.

What does the future hold for the jet engines of tomorrow? The demand for aviation continues to increase, and while aviation accounts for only 2% of greenhouse gas emissions, the emphasis more than ever revolves around the environment and reducing the impact on the climate. Engines produce far lower emissions, are quieter and consume less fuel than ever before. New materials are being developed in the quest for greater efficiency. As fossil fuels become scarce, research into alternative fuels is already being conducted. Whatever the future may hold, aviation will continue to enable people to expand their horizons through travel around the world.

Gloster Meteor T7 at Newark Air Museum

Eight prototype Meteors were built and various engines were tried out in them. After the first flight piloted by Michael Daunt, further development moved to Newmarket Heath and, later, to Gloster's site at Moreton Valence in Gloucestershire.

Mike Daunt getting ready to fly the F.9/40 Meteor. He survived being sucked into the engine inlet

John Crosby-Warren (test pilot); Michael Daunt (test pilot); Frank McKenna (general manager, Gloucester aircraft); Frank Whittle and George Carter (chief designer) in front of the first F9/40

Whittle-made engines were used for the first time on the 12th of June, 1943 in DG205/G. The Meteor F1 first flew from Moreton Valence on 12th January, 1944, a few weeks after the German Me 262's first flight. The Meteor was equipped with four 20mm cannons and was using Whittle engines. By this time, Rolls Royce had taken over the manufacture of the jet engine.

Frank Whittle and his son Ian (A senior pilot for Cathay Pacific) in front of the Meteor

Frank Whittle had become even more dissatisfied with Rovers. He had to wait a long time for the drawings of the W2 engine. Then they began to ignore the terms of reference and started to alter details. Adrian Lombard attempted to develop the W2 into a production quality design dispensing with Whittle's reverse flow burners. Whittle became frustrated with Rovers and made no attempt to hide his displeasure and the Chairman of Rovers, S.B.Wilkes found him very difficult to deal with. Stanley Hooker was asked to go to Clitheroe where the engine was being built to try and sort out the differences between the two men. He discovered that Rovers had made major changes to the fuel and combustion systems. Whittle was furious at the changes Wilkes wished to make. He felt that it wasn't the time to make major changes but Wilkes persisted. Rover had all the facilities for making the jet engine but they had started on the redesign of the W2 engine. When he returned to Derby and told Lord Hives of the situation, they both decided to go to Clitheroe to meet Wilkes over dinner at the Swan and Royal in the High Street. The three of them were long standing friends. They discussed the problems that had arisen and Lord Hives offered to take over the jet business in exchange for the tank engine factory in Nottingham.

That evening, he sent the telegram to Whittle – "We've got your baby".

It was the best news Whittle could have received. He was so relieved that it felt as though a weight had been lifted off his shoulders.

In 1943, Rolls Royce took over the manufacture of the jet engine.

At the end of March 1941, the engine was despatched to Glosters and was installed in E 28/39 for taxiing trials on 7th April 1941. Whittle made a few runs in it reaching a speed of 60mph as did Gerry Sayer, Gloster's chief test pilot on the following day. He also made several hops when the aircraft was airborne for a few seconds. It is not hard for one to imagine the sheer sense of pride and overpowering joy which filled Sir Frank Whittle on the 15th of May at 7.40.p.m. when the first British jet aircraft, the Gloster E 28/39 'Pioneer' made its first flight at RAF Cranwell. So many people had tried to deter him, telling him that an aircraft powered by a jet engine was impossible and improbable but his tenacity and drive enabled him to overcome these criticisms. Even so, before take off, he was filled with self doubt. Would the engine fulfil its potential? He need not have worried as this first flight lasted seventeen minutes reaching a maximum speed of 545 km/h. Within days, it was reaching 600 km/h. Many wonder how Frank felt during this first flight. No-one will ever know what truly went through his mind but he must have felt some pride and sense of achievement as the E 28/39 flew above him.

It was a thrilling experience. It was clear that we would not be short of thrust when we used the permissible maximum of 16,000 rpm. Also, the complete lack of vibration, the big reduction of noise when compared with traditional aircraft, the excellent view from the cockpit and the simplicity of the controls all added up to an impressive combination of characteristics.

The aircraft was then returned to Lutterworth for further development. After further tests, the Ministry of Aircraft cleared the engine for ten hours of flight testing. The aircraft was then transported to R.A.F. Cranwell with great secrecy and flew on the 15th of May, a flight that lasted 17 minutes. Despite its success, the flight had no publicity and even people stationed at Cranwell at the time did not realise or appreciate the importance of the occasion. But then the country was at war. England was fearing a German invasion at the time. Unusual things happening were accepted but there were many who did appreciate its significance. Dr Harold Roxbee Cox, now Lord Kings Norton, wrote at the time, "Before Whittle, the gas turbine had been regarded like other turbines as a machine for supplying shaft power. He recognised it as the ideal means of providing jet propulsion for aircraft."

Whatever must Frank Whittle have been feeling during the first successful flight of the jet engine after so much hard work, trial, error and correction?

The E 28/39 flew again in February 1942, this time powered by the W1A engine.

All aircraft, apart from gliders, use some form of propulsion to keep them moving forwards: either a propeller or a jet engine. Both depend on Sir Isaac Newton's third and best known law of motion, which states that for every *action,* there must be an equal and opposite *reaction*. The propeller and the jet engine push air backwards to produce a force which pushes the aircraft forwards.

When Frank Whittle was a cadet at RAF Cranwell all aircraft used propellers that were rotated by piston engines. The top speed of RAF fighters was about 150mph at 5000 feet. Frank Whittle realised that for an aircraft to attain greater speeds and fly greater distances, it must fly higher than 35,000 feet above sea level where the atmosphere is thinner, so you don't encounter as much air resistance. An example in his thesis states that if an aircraft reaches 60 mph when flying at sea level, then it will reach 300 mph when flying above 35,000 feet, using the same amount of thrust. He even imagined aircraft flying faster than 500mph.

He knew he would have to tackle the problem that piston-engine aircraft cannot cope at high altitude because the air is too thin. Although a supercharger could be used to pressurize the air before it entered the pistons it would still use up too much energy.

So he wrote about creating a new engine, using a similar idea to that of the rocket, ejecting gases at high speeds from a nozzle - but a rocket would not be efficient enough. Then he looked at another principle, the steam turbine - but this would be too heavy. He also looked at using a gas turbine to drive a propeller, but he knew that there was a limit to the speed of propeller-driven aircraft because the tips of the blades become supersonic. He kept working on the problem and, 18 months later, had the idea of using a gas turbine, not to turn a propeller, but for jet propulsion.

The idea of jet propulsion can be demonstrated through the use of any party balloon. When inflated, the pressure within the balloon is greater than outside of the balloon. If it is tied, the air inside pushes equally in all directions and the balloon will remain at rest.

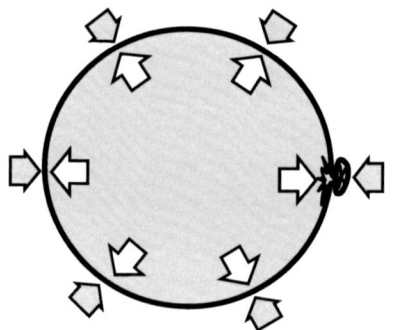

All Forces Balanced

When the knot is undone the air will escape into the atmosphere. This causes an imbalance of forces within the balloon in such a way that the balloon moves forward. This effect is the result of Newton's Third Law of Motion. (N.B. Sir Isaac Newton was born in Lincolnshire in 1642. The theories he created more than 300 years ago are vital to the working of the jet engine.)

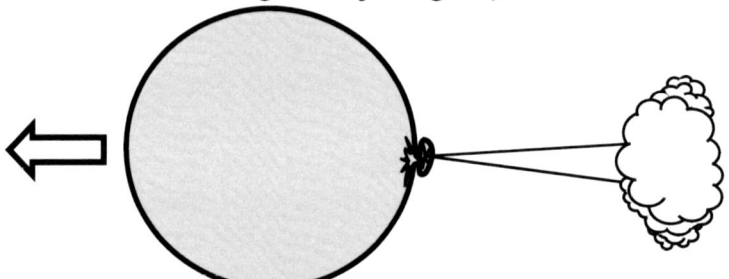

Imbalance of forces creates thrust

Hero's Engine

A balloon cannot fly very far because the pressurized air inside it soon runs out. The air must be replaced in some way for jet propulsion to continue. One of the earliest examples of continuous jet propulsion was the engine designed by Hero of Alexandria in 150BC. This engine made use of steam pressure within a vessel, which was released through nozzles splaying in an outwards direction producing a jet-like reaction to turn it. As the steam escaped through the nozzles, more steam was produced in a boiler underneath so it could run for a long time.

Frank Whittle thought of the different ways in which a continuous flow of hot gas could be ejected from a jet pipe. Eventually, he got the idea for the jet engine, which he patented in January 1930. The diagram below is not exactly like his first engine, but it shows the main parts a jet engine to explain how it works.

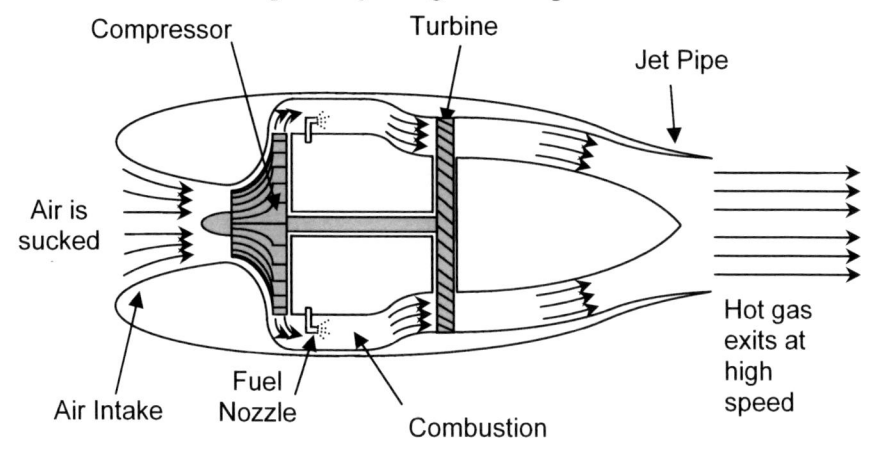

The jet engine works in four simple steps:
    Step 1: Air is sucked into the air intake.
    Step 2: The air is squeezed by the compressor into a smaller space so that its pressure increases.

Step 3: Fuel is sprayed into the combustion chamber and the fuel/air mixture is ignited so it becomes very hot.

Step 4: This hot air expands and rushes through the turbine, making it spin, and then out of the jet pipe at high speed creating the necessary force to go forward.

Frank Whittle's brilliant idea was to add the turbine, which he connected to the compressor with a shaft. When the hot air turns the turbine it makes the compressor turn, which squeezes in more air and the whole process keeps going.

One advantage of a jet engine is that the compressor and turbine keep turning in the same direction, so it runs very smoothly. In a piston engine, the pistons keep changing direction, which causes more vibration. Also in a piston engine, the steps of compression, combustion and expansion take place intermittently in each piston, so each produces power on only one of its four strokes. In a jet engine the cycle is continuous so it is more efficient. Lastly, by not using a propeller, jet aircraft can fly faster - the RAF's Typhoon fighter can fly at 1350 mph or twice the speed of sound.

We will now look at the parts of the engine in more detail and some of the engineering challenges that Frank Whittle had to overcome

The purpose of the compressor is to squeeze the air into a smaller volume and increase its pressure. It rotates at a very high speed of 20000 rpm or more. There are two types of compressor: centrifugal and axial. A centrifugal compressor sucks in air at the middle and hurls it outwards at high speed into a small space where the pressure rises. An axial compressor has a series of multi-bladed fans, each one pushing the air backwards and squeezing it a bit more.

It is important to squeeze the air as much as possible. When Frank Whittle had his idea for the jet engine he said the compressor would need to increase the pressure by about 4 times. Other scientists and engineers thought this would be impossible, but he designed a centrifugal compressor that would do it. Compressors in modern engines for civil airliners can increase the pressure by more than 40 times.

Centrifugal compressor and turbine of Frank Whittle's first test engine
Picture courtesy of Rolls Royce

When the air is squeezed it gets hotter. Increasing the air pressure and temperature before it is mixed with fuel makes the engine much more efficient. The fuel consumed to produce the thrust is lower so the aircraft can travel further more economically.

The compressed and heated air enters the combustion chamber, where it mixes with fuel supplied by nozzles. For the combustion chamber to work at its optimum, the fuel must be burned at the appropriate air-to-fuel ratio: approximately 15 parts air to 1 part fuel. The mixture of air and fuel is ignited. This creates heat that expands the gas and forces it from the rear of the chamber at high speed.

Frank Whittle had to satisfy certain conditions to allow the combustion chamber to work correctly. To create enough thrust, the fuel has to be burnt at a very high rate. He wanted to burn more fuel in a much smaller space than anyone had achieved before. This is why the air needs to be squeezed by the compressor, so that there are lots of small molecules of oxygen in a very small space. There is then a higher chance of the oxygen and fuel molecules colliding together with enough energy to create a successful reaction. He had to make sure that combustion was stable so that the air rushing through the combustion chamber didn't blow out the flame.

When the hot gases leave the combustion chamber they pass into the turbine. The turbine consists of one or more rotating disks with blades arranged around the edge. The high velocity air pushes on the blades, which makes the disk rotate like the wind makes the sails of a windmill turn - only much faster (more than 20000 rpm). The turbine and compressor are joined together with a shaft so that the turbine turns the compressor. One of the main problems with the turbine is withstanding the high temperature as described below.

Compressor and turbine of Frank Whittle's first flight engine
Picture courtesy of Rolls Royce

Frank Whittle's first design for a jet engine is called a *turbojet*. He also had the idea for a *turbofan* engine, which is used on most aircraft today. In this engine, the turbine is also used to drive a fan located at the front of the engine. Some of the air from the fan goes through a duct, which bypasses the compressor, combustion chamber and turbine before mixing with the hot gases from the jet pipe. This makes the engine quieter and more fuel efficient.

Most components of the engine are made from alloys. An alloy is a combination of different metals, which provide desirable characteristics. One alloy is stainless steel which is mostly iron, but doesn't corrode or stain because chromium is also added. Alloys for making engine components must be strong, hard wearing, work at very high temperature, survive rapid temperature changes, not corrode easily or shatter and be cost effective.

One reason why the Air Ministry initially turned down Frank Whittle's proposal for a jet engine was that they thought no alloys could possibly withstand the high temperatures. There were none at the time, but Whittle was confident they could be developed and he was right. In his first engine, the hot gas from the combustion chamber was at about 780°C. In modern engines the gas in the combustion chamber reaches 2000°C.

When the turbine is working fully the force on each blade could be equal to the weight of an elephant. The blades were made from special nickel alloys to withstand these conditions. The picture below shows the turbine from Frank Whittle's first engine which failed under the high forces and temperatures during testing.

Turbine failure during testing of Frank Whittle's first engine
Picture courtesy of Rolls Royce

Modern turbine blades are often manufactured by investment casting. First a metal mould is created, in which wax blades are cast. These are then coated with silica slurry. The wax is melted to leave a hollow silica mould into which a molten alloy is poured to set. The silica mould is then broken off to leave the metal blade, which is then polished and trimmed to make sure it is correct.

A problem with blades is that they contain many tiny crystals, known as grains. The boundaries between these grains could potentially lead to cracks in the blade. Fortunately modern casting now allows us to cool a cast blade better, so that we can create blades that have grain boundaries running along the blade or have no grains at all. The latter are known as single crystal turbine blades. Turbine blades are surrounded by very hot gas that has just left the combustion chamber. The temperature of the gas can be as high as 1600°C, which is higher than the melting point or the blade material, so they need cooling. This can be done in two ways. The first is where some air from the compressor is pumped through the inside of the turbine blade. Although the air tapped off from the compressor is hot it is still a lot cooler than the gas leaving the combustion chamber.

The second way is where the turbine has holes drilled into it on the leading edge. This means that when the cooling air is pumped through it, a thin film of relatively cool air is created over the blade, stopping the hot gas getting to it and causing thermal damage.

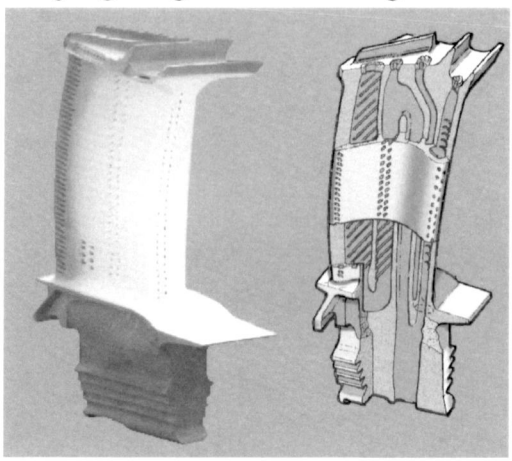

Copyright Rolls Royce plc

Air passes through cooling channels inside the turbine blade

Because of the possibility of an invasion, the Government started taking steps to protect national treasures and records and made plans to send some of them to Canada. This is where they were considering sending the plans and records of the jet engine. But it happened that the American General 'Hap' Arnold was visiting Britain at this time and persuaded the British Government to send them to America instead. This was before Pearl Harbour and the Americans had not yet entered the Second World War. The Government agreed to the proposal saying that they could develop the jet engine for civil aircraft for which the Americans paid the British Government 900,000 dollars. A complete set of drawings and three members of Power Jets travelled to the General Electric Company's turbine factory at Lynn, Massachusetts. Before this, three of GEC's engineers had visited the Lutterworth plant. One of them claimed that they had had that equipment for years and he couldn't think why none of them had thought about putting the combustion chamber between the compressor and the turbine.

In May, 1942, Frank Whittle went to America in a flying boat to discuss the future development of the jet engine. The Americans took to him straight away, calling him a loveable little man. They had been expecting a typical public school type Brit instead they met the small, friendly intelligent man who earned their respect. They recognised the genius in the man and appreciated the way he was ready to help others in any way he could.

Engineers began to think that the jet engine could have other uses than powering aircraft. The directors of Ruston and Hornsby in Lincoln saw the future of jet engines and they were one of the firms that invited a team from Power Jets to advise them on the use of gas turbines. There were some heavy snowfalls in the 1940s and the local railway asked Power Jets to clear the snow from the lines which they did very efficiently. Unfortunately they removed most of the ballast between the lines as well. When they were asked to help clear the roads, they not only removed the snow but the road surface as well. But, it was aviation where the jet engine was most successful and for which Frank Whittle developed it. It transformed aviation but Frank Whittle came so very close to abandoning the project.

Whittle has gone down in history as being the first man to patent a jet engine but he was not the first man to see one lift off the ground. A German, Hans von Ohain was working on a similar project. Where Whittle had little encouragement, von Ohain's was undertaken in very different conditions. He and his assistant, Max Hahn were at Gottingen University when they were approached by Ernst Heinkel who backed their research. While Frank worked in a shed using reclaimed scrap metal, the two Germans were given first class facilities and a huge amount of funding.

Hans von Ohain

In April, 1937, Whittle had successfully run his first bed engine but the Air Ministry still would not accept is design. Two years later, the Germans were trying out the first flight of the He178. The flight may only have lasted a few seconds but it flew. By then, even the Italians had launched a jet powered aircraft although it was not a turbojet.

Von Ohain said that if the Air Ministry had taken Whittle seriously at the start, there wouldn't have been a Second World War. The air superiority it would have given the British would have dissuaded Hitler who believed that power in the air was all important. As it was, Hitler did not like the idea of jet power so He178 and He 280 were never accepted or used during the war.

Max Hahn said that when Whittle's copyright ran out, every technical library in Germany had a copy. Ohain and Whittle met after the war and became good friends. They decided to share the honours for the first jet engine between them.

At the end of the war, Britain led the world in jet propulsion. Whittle wanted Power Jets to continue a research programme but the firm was nationalised and prevented from building engines and so he left the firm that had dominated his life for so many years. He received no payment for the firm or for any of the work he had done other than his RAF salary. Later he received £100,000 as an award from the Royal Commission on awards to inventors, an enormous sum of money, worth more than two million pounds today. He wanted his Reactionaries, the men who had worked with him, to receive an award as well but this was refused because they had been paid for the work they did. Whittle never forgot the men who had worked with him and he shared some of his award with them.

The years of strain had taken their toll on his health. He spent several months in hospital and retired from the RAF through ill health.

He received the KBE for his work and was knighted by King George V1, the first Old Cranwellian to be knighted.

Sir Frank Whittle, KBE

Meanwhile we can see evidence of the way the jet engine has changed the world in so many ways.

I first met Sir Frank Whittle in 1943 as a 16 year old engineering apprentice with Power Jets Ltd at Whetstone near Leicester. I was a very junior employee. We became firm friends and I acted as an agent on a number of projects.

I was both fortunate and privileged to have been so closely associated with Sir Frank Whittle, a wonderful friend and a man who became the greatest engineer of the twentieth century. He was a modern genius and had many other attributes than just sheer technical brilliance. He had courage, determination, dignity and generosity together with an infectious sense of humour.

Sir Frank was an inspirational team leader and a gentleman. He expected commitment, dedication and loyalty from his colleagues. He did not suffer fools gladly. He possessed a wonderful personality and charm that enabled him to mix so easily with any class of society.

His memory was quite exceptional. His anecdotes and stories of his flying days at Cranwell reduced everyone to fits of laughter.

Sir Frank was exceedingly proud of this country of ours. He never stopped talking about it. He retained his British nationality (and his English accent) although he lived in America.

He had tremendous respect for the R.A.F. which he held in high esteem and considered it to be the finest service anywhere in the world. He always gave credit both privately and publicly to the training he received both as an apprentice and as a cadet at Cranwell for his success but his greatest pride was for his family.

He was a family man, a wonderful human being, a great friend and my life has been enriched by knowing him,
Roy Fowkes, a Reactionary.

At home with his wife Dorothy and his sons, David and Ian

HANDS ON- Being the pilot of an aircraft is a rewarding experience and a demanding one. The training never stops. I have been flying for 20 years and have over 6,000 hours flying time.
Today's pilots have aircraft that fly themselves and are full of technology to assist the pilot. However, decisions still need to be made and technology is used, coupled with the pilot's experience, to make the right decision. Military aircraft fly at low levels where they carry out high 'G' manoeuvres such as tight turns and often fly in close formation especially for air-to-air refuelling. All my flying is

gentle and as smooth as possible to make sure that the passengers are as comfortable as they can be. When turning, for example, the bank angle is kept to a minimum and the rate at which it is applied is very gentle.

Jet engines are much more powerful than piston engines meaning that aircraft can be bigger and fly faster and higher. This reduces cost to the operator. Jet engines require less servicing than a piston engine. Because the piston engine has a propeller, more power is required. The bigger the propeller, the less time there is between servicing which results in increased costs. In today's world, economic and social demand means that speed and weight outperform the lighter and slower performance of the piston engine.

Turboprop engines are efficient for short flights betweens cities but they do not have the performance to fly long distances. With the piston engines, the more power required, the more propellers or bigger propellers are required. The long range flights take longer in a turboprop. It is OK to have a military patrol or transport aircraft with turbo props as they are not required to make a profit. Commercial organisations want to carry greater loads over greater distances quickly and cheaply. Jet aircraft fly higher and quicker and carrying more loads over greater distances so are more efficient.

Why were the ash clouds so dangerous to aircraft? The ash produced by the volcanic eruption was bad news for engines. The ash particles (powdered rocks) melt inside the hot part of the engine and solidify in the cooler part. This causes the flow of air through the engine to become disrupted and the engine to stall and fail. Flying through the ash cloud also damages the skin surface of the aeroplane, particularly the edges of the wings, tail plane and windows. This is due to friction and you can compare it to washing your face with sand paper. The ash also blocks holes in the aircraft that are used to provide air data to the instruments – bad news.

On a Virgin Atlantic Boeing 747-400, the Captain and I are responsible for the safe operation of the aircraft and the safety of all passengers and crew. We operate the aircraft in accordance with

Virgin Atlantic Standard Operating Procedures (SOPs). Our job is to ensure that everybody on the aircraft, passengers and crew travel to their destination as safely and as comfortably as possible. In the event of an emergency, the pilots will deal with the aircraft, the technical issues and Air Traffic Control (ATC) while keeping the crew and passengers informed. The cabin crew's main responsibility is the safety of the passengers, especially if an evacuation on the ground is ordered by the pilots. They have to get 450 passengers and 17crew off the aircraft in less than 90 seconds. All due to Whittle.
    Jonathon Williams– Pilot – Boeing 747, Virgin Airline.

Picture by kind permission of Virgin Atlantic

 I am the XO (Executive Officer) on XI Squadron at RAF Coningsby. I fly the RAF's newest fighter, the Eurofighter Typhoon. It is an absolute privilege to fly an aircraft with such immense power and fantastic handling. I am responsible to the Squadron Commander for ensuring the smooth operation of the Squadron from Operations to Engineering and life support. I fly mostly in the instructor role, teaching and leading junior pilots, bringing them to a Combat Ready standard. There is a lot to learn. It is important to study tactics and doctrine and learn from others to make us as effective as possible. We spend a lot of time discussing Flight Safety as military flying is such an unforgiving environment we try to be as safe as possible whilst remaining an effective military asset.

    The Typhoon is swing-role. It can perform Air to Air and Air to Ground missions. We fly mostly Air to Air missions at the moment since that is our standing commitment. The Tornado GR4 is performing well in Afghanistan in the Air to Ground role. A typical Air to Air mission will involve flying with 4 Typhoons against a number of similar adversaries. We fly sorties, mostly over the North Sea to avoid confliction with civilian traffic and to give us the flexibility for high performance manoeuvring. The scenario for the mission is important, the Squadron Intelligence Officer will brief this. It will normally involve protecting an area or valuable asset against a simulated surface to air missile sites. A typical sortie will normally be one hour, forty minutes but the planning, briefing, flying and debriefing will normally last about seven hours.

    I joined the Royal Air Force in 1994 after tasting the flying experience with the University Air Squadron. I had a short spell prior to starting RAFC Cranwell as an accountant in London which was fine intellectually but I had the flying bug. The lure of aviation drove me into signing on the dotted line of the RAF. I joined as a Navigator since places for pilots in 1992 were extremely limited. I had great fun flying all the training aircraft as a student navigator, eventually ending up on the Tornado F3 based at RAF Leuchars.

    By this time, the RAF were very short of pilots and I was offered a place as a student pilot, albeit right back at the beginning of the flying training system on the Slingsby Firefly. I progressed from the Firefly and Tucano to the Hawk and, at the end of Tactical Weapons at RAF Valley, I was posted to the Harrier GR7. The Harrier was a fantastic aircraft to fly, tricky, demanding but rewarding at the same time. One of the best attributes of the aircraft besides taking off and landing from short runway surfaces was the ability to land and take off vertically. It was always challenging landing vertically, not least when operating from one of the Royal Navy's aircraft carriers. Hovering alongside HMS Invincible at 100 feet with people standing on 'Goofers' 30 feet from you, at your level watching you as you manly struggled to place the jet in the right place was a surreal experience. I was lucky enough to see Operations in Iraq and Afghanistan on the harrier, a fantastic aircraft. It will be missed.

Prior to flying the Typhoon, all the aircraft I flew were single engine. With the safety of the aircraft reliant on one engine only, they had to be good to give the pilot reassurance. The Harrier's engine, the Pegasus, was extremely well engineered and robust. In the hover at 100 feet, the pilot only had 1.5 seconds to eject from the aircraft should there have been a hiccup with the Pegasus. After the Harrier, I flew the F16 on exchange with the Royal Netherlands Air Force. It was a good stepping stone to flying the Typhoon. The F16s large wing area allowed it to glide should the engine fail. Luckily, in the life of the F16 which is far the most highly produced and exported modern fighter, it has only happened on a few occasions. The F16 variant which I flew had the Pratt and Witney 220 engine which developed an enormous amount of thrust especially in reheat. It enabled the F16 to carry a large payload when taking part in foreign operations.

The Typhoon is powered by 2 EJ200 engines which are the cutting edge of fighter engine design. They produce 13 thousand pounds of thrust in reheat. When flying the aircraft, it is very hard to slow down since the engines are so powerful and the aircraft so slippery. On take off in re-heat, unless the aircraft is 30 degrees nose-up or more, it will go supersonic. Descending from 42 thousand feet with both engines at idle, the aircraft will go supersonic unless you slow down with airbrake or by manoeuvring the aircraft using a split-S manoeuvre. The aircraft easily pulls to 9g. Normally this would be painful to the pilot but the life support for the aircraft has been well designed. The pilot is dressed in full cover g protection suits and systems including socks. The aircraft also forces air into the pilot. This is called pressure breathing. All this remarkable *technology helps prevent the pilot from blackout or G- loss of consciousness much longer than it would when flying a traditional fighter aircraft.*

The performance take-off of the Typhoon involves rotating the aircraft in reheat at take-off speed to an almost vertical climb out. On a recent foreign detachment, at night, with both engines in reheat, the aircraft looked like the Space Shuttle leaving Cape Canaveral. I am lucky to fly such a high performing, state of the art aircraft. It puts a smile on my face every time I get airborne. All due to Whittle.

Squadron Leader Rupert Joel, Executive Officer XI Squadron. Royal Air Force, Coningsby.

Women in the Development of the Jet Engine

Since the creation of the jet engine, there have been a number of developments which have improved its efficiency. They are still being carried out, including the work of Professor Dame Ann Dowling, a professor of mechanical engineering at the University of Cambridge. Currently, the focus of her research and development is low-emission combustion and quieter engines.

There have been many women in the past who have also had an input. Anne Burns (1915-2001) played a huge part in testing the structure of airframes during and after the Second World War. She joined the Royal Aircraft Establishment in 1940 and by 1954 was appointed Principal Scientific Officer. Following this, she received the Queen's Commendation for valuable services in the air after flying in an unpressurised Comet jet airliner to try and investigate what was stopping the plane from functioning correctly. She was well known for her knowledge of turbulence, mainly for her work with Clear Air Turbulence in the regions where jet airliners fly, a fantastic woman in the development of safety of jet flight.

There were also women who were made famous for flying. Anne Burns won a number of awards for her gliding. Amy Johnson was made famous by her attempt to break the world record for flying from the UK to Australia. The record for this flight originally stood at 15 days but Amy was determined to beat it. On May 5th, 1930, she set off on her trip to break the world record. Due to mechanical failures caused by the awful weather, she finally landed in Darwin, Australia. She was still made famous after being the first woman to fly solo to Australia. She won a number of other awards with her biplane 'Jason', a De Havilland Moth that had cost her father and Lord Wakefield £600.

Other early female pilots were Jean Batten and Jacqueline Cochran. Jean Batten was one of the most successful aviators from New Zealand. In 1933, she made the flight from England to Australia in 14 days and 22 hours. In 1935, she became the first woman to make the return flight, managing this in an astounding 17 days. She broke other records in including flying from England to Brazil in 1936. Jacqueline Cochran was the first woman to fly faster than the speed of sound.

So what does the future hold for the jet engine? In these times of rising fuel costs and climate change, increased efficiency is the main goal being discussed by aircraft engineers, reflecting Frank Whittle's own thoughts. Always the pioneer, he researched fuels for his engines which he wanted to be non smoking to reduce pollution. Fuel research will doubtless continue in the future as existing fuels become harder to find and more expensive. Climate change ensures that less polluting fuels will be favoured.

New fuel developments will also allow for higher thermal efficiency as they can increase the temperature in the combustion chamber of the engine, resulting in greater expansion in the jet of gas which powers the aircraft. A fuel that, gram for gram, produces more heat energy when burnt would, therefore, not only be more efficient but would allow faster flight, possibly without the problems of increased pollution and noise. These advances could be used by both the military and commercial sectors.

The temperature inside the engine is controlled to a large extent by the materials, so the discovery of new alloys will play a huge part in the way forward. They could allow engines to be built that are stronger, lighter and more efficient than ever before. New materials could make engine casings lighter for example so less fuel would be needed whilst staying rigid so that the shape and air flow are maintained.

The future may also hold changes for the use of the jet engine. Jet propelled cars and back packs are consigned to science fiction but they may become possible and affordable. The new frontier of space tourism may also benefit from the use of the jet engine. The rocket engine relies on carrying, not only it own fuel supplies, but also oxygen which means it can only be used for a comparatively short time. If a jet engine could be used for the first stages of the journey, then less of the precious oxygen would be used up, meaning that longer flights itself could be undertaken.

Whatever the future may hold for the jet engine, one thing is certain. Without Frank Whittle, none of it would have been possible.

A.B.

Sir Frank followed in his father's footsteps as an Engineer. His experiences as an Apprentice and then a Flight Cadet at the RAF College ultimately provided the rounded engineer, pilot and officer that he became. Cranwell gave Whittle the opportunity to distinguish himself in practically everything he did.

Sir Frank showed the true spirit of aviation, determination and flair of an officer cadet at the College when he flew aerobatics in an Armstrong Whitworth Siskin – an aircraft which was not designed for aerobatics. During one aerobatic display, he was the first Cadet to perform a "Bunt" (the first half of an outside loop where a steepening dive finishes up inverted) in a Siskin at 1,500ft which was a very low level at which to perform such a manoeuvre.

A Siskin

Sir Frank's individuality was shown in his 4th term thesis which was entitled *"Future Developments in Aircraft Design"*. He had a naturally enquiring mind which made him ask searching questions, some of which his tutor (Prof O S Sinnatt) did not understand.

Sir Frank Whittle is still an excellent role model for today's officer cadets. As his portrait gazes down from the East end of the Dining Room in College Hall, it reminds Cadets of the qualities he had of initiative, determination and application which are key to training as an officer cadet. His training and career as a pilot shows how beneficial even a basic understanding of engineering and the principles of flight are to the student pilot, and this should provide inspiration for success in their future career.

The RAF College's first knighted cadet, this 'son of Cranwell' proved himself as an officer and a gentleman and showed that it doesn't matter what one's background is, because with determination and application, anything can be achieved.

Air Commodore Paul Oborn
Commandant of the RAF College, Cranwell